Home Remedies

By **RUTH FLAXMAN**

ILLUSTRATED BY
M. YEROW

A PERIGEE BOOK

Perigee Books
are published by
G. P. Putnam's Sons
200 Madison Avenue
New York, New York 10016

Library of Congress Catalog Card Number 81-52586
ISBN 0-399-50685-3

Cover & book design by Michael Meyerowitz
Front cover photograph by Ron Boszko

Printed in the United States of America.
First Perigee printing, 1982.

To my wonderful family: Nath, Evelyn, Marian, Lee, Caroline, Gary, and Laura.

ACKNOWLEDGMENTS

I would like to thank all the people who were so kind to give their time, thought, and tips. Special thanks to Sasha Futran-Rivas and Janice Insolia. Thanks also to Renee Bernbach, Sarah Black, Buck Buchanen, Ann Burch, Wendy Caplin, Richard Carlson, Luna Carne-Ross, Jim Charlton, Munishree Chitrabanu, Rona Deme, Diamond Crystal Salt Company, Rose Dorsay, Evelyn Ellenbogen, Sara Lyn Esh, Annette Exner, Ivy Fischer, Jonathan Firstenberg, Annick Flaxman, Caroline Flaxman, Debbie Froelich, Constance Gill, Belsada Hansel, Brook Hedick, Judy Hinger, Johnson & Johnson Baby Products Company, Bertha Jackter, Beredine Jocelyn, Annunciata Kent, Tobi Krutt, Dorothy Lara-Braud, Tim Metevier, Nelle Morphy, Judy Myers, Victor Navasky, Patricia Neely, Dave Nehila, Lucy Pellegrini, Peter Pickow, Antoine Raffoul, Jason Shulman, Rudolf Steiner, Wesley Sutton, Ruth Taller, Joe Tenga, Naomi Wexler, and Herb Wise.

CONTENTS

9

10

FOREWORD

This delightful and entertaining book offers a wealth of helpful hints collected from a variety of sources. The author's recommendations are usually inexpensive and take advantage of giving nature time to heal, while easing discomfort.

The folk wisdom from which most of these notions are derived suggests the many natural products that have led to modern medicines. We know that the Egyptians made soothing, antiseptic balms of honey and resin. The Greeks knew the sleep-producing qualities of wine and opium, both of which were exported from Cyprus to Egypt more than three thousand years ago. Ephedrin for asthma has been used in India for at least as long. Imagine the wonder of seventeenth-century European patients and physicians when Spanish travelers to the New World sent home Colchis tree bark, which contains colchecine, to cure gout; the bark of the cinchona tree, whose extract quinine relieves the fever of malaria; and the coca leaf which contains the stimulant and anesthetic cocaine.

Explorers, scientists and physicians in the eighteenth and nineteenth centuries continued the search for other medicinal plants. Folk cures were sought out and tried, and when effective, the active ingredients were identified.

In the eighteenth century, the English physician Withering suggested that the leaf of the Foxglove plant could treat heart failure—and indeed it can because it contains digitalis. Willow bark, long brewed into a tea to relieve rheumatism, was found by the German chemist Bayer to contain acetylsalicylic acid. He later synthesized it and called it aspirin. The study of these and other natural products led to the modern era of medicine when in the 1920s insulin was identified and then the green mold of penicillin found on bread and cheese was recognized as a bacteria-killing agent.

Most illnesses are brief and self-limited. It is ironic perhaps that medicine is most effective not for the nagging ache or minor cold but for life-threatening conditions such as pneumonia or heart failure. Yet much time is lost and money spent on temporary discomfort. The suggestions in this book may be just what the reader needs to ease the distress of a brief illness. We all know that good health depends on a moderate diet, plenty of exercise, restraint in the use of alcohol and salt, and the absolute refusal to smoke cigarettes. A caution, however, for the fever that continues, the headache that will not go away, the recurrent rash or the persistent lump or for any symptom that lasts more than a few days—you should seek the advice of your physician. Used wisely, many of these hints can be quite helpful and who knows, one might contain the secret of another cure.

David Bennahum, M.D.,
Presbyterian Hospital Center,
Albuquerque, New Mexico.

AUTHOR'S PREFACE

In the United States, which has been industrialized for several generations, the lore of "house medicine" has been largely neglected and lost. This is the medicine for ailments that are not serious enough for a doctor's care, but that can be treated effectively with items one finds around the house. By no means are these remedies a replacement for a doctor's care. They are for the little maladies that afflict everyone from time to time: coughs, aches and pains, cuts, bruises, sore throats, rashes, dry skin, etc.

Without exception, all the immigrant cultures that came to America had their own house medicine. For decades here it has been "better," more "modern," to ignore the old remedies and consult a doctor instead. In the other cultures there would be, in addition to the doctor, one or more people who knew exactly what to do for minor ailments and whom everyone consulted. My grandmother, who emigrated from the Austro-Hungarian Empire, was such a person. The people in the village where she lived came to her for advice. She would take every opportunity to compare and exchange remedies with other experts, both from her own and from other villages. There was no charge for such advice.

When my grandmother came to America, she made every effort to be a "modern" woman. She adopted American ways as fast as she could, but when it came to the house medicine, she found her remedies were as effective and far less expensive than those of a doctor. So she handed them down to her children and grandchildren. Even more important to me than the specific remedies was her attitude toward medicine: See first if there is something one can do for oneself, but for serious illnesses, or those that might be serious, do not hesitate to go to a doctor. Or if a person already *has* a serious illness and is under the care of a doctor, the doctor should be consulted before trying these remedies. But most of the ailments mentioned in this book will go away or be alleviated by the simple means.

In preparing this book I have been extremely fortunate to have found experts in house medicine from various cultures and to have received excellent tips from many people. These remedies are by no means all old. Ban Roll-On, for example, which works like magic on a poison ivy rash, was given to me by a pediatrician who found it effective on patients for years.

There is a general principle to keep in mind: Doctors know that not every medicine will work for every person. If one does not work, another might, or perhaps two or three in combination. The same applies to home remedies. So, for example, if one hangover or hiccup remedy does not work for you, try another until you find the one that suits you.

I have collected, compared, evaluated, and distilled hundreds of tips, and had a lot of fun doing it. I hope the reader gets as much enjoyment from trying them as I did in putting them together. Perhaps this will encourage you to record some of your own experiences. I would be very pleased if you would send me tips you have tried and found useful.

14

Home Remedies

ARTHRITIS

Arthritis sufferers should try sleeping every night in a sleeping bag. The even, overall warmth helps the morning stiffness.

Various folk medicine traditions use celery to ease the pain of arthritis. This one is easy to make:

Boil 1 ounce celery seeds in 1 pint water until only about ½ pint is left. Take a dosage of 1 teaspoon a day.

ASTHMA

INDIAN ASTHMA RELIEF RECIPE

Place 1 entire egg in a wineglass and cover with lemon juice. Leave for twelve hours to soften the shell. Remove shell, and beat yolk and white together. Add honey equal to the amount of lemon juice. Bring mixture to a boil, and when it starts to thicken, remove from heat. Bottle when cool and use as needed. Recommended dosage is 1 teaspoon, morning and night.

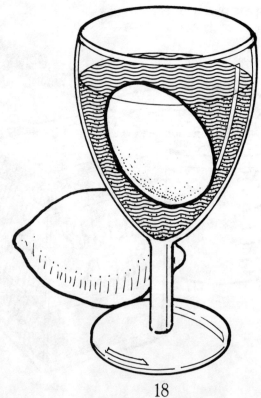

BREATH

Sweeten the breath by chewing:

> a stick of cinnamon
> cloves
> nutmeg
> parsley
> mace
> licorice root
> mint leaves
> rosemary
> cardamom or caraway seeds

For onion and garlic breath, eat a slice of lemon with salt on it.

The English Renaissance herbalist John Gerard advised for bad breath:

"The distilled water of the floures of Rosemary being drunke at morning and evening first and last, taketh away the stench of the mouth and breath, and maketh it very sweet, if there be added thereto, to steep or infuse for certaine daies, a few Cloves, Mace, Cinnamon, and a little Anise seed."

COLDS

This contemporary home recipe for a cold incorporates some cold-inhibiting ingredients used since ancient times:

Into the juice of 1 lemon mix ⅛ teaspoon cayenne pepper, 1 minced garlic clove, and 1000 mg. vitamin C. Drink it straight or diluted with water or camomile tea.

For colds, make hot lemonade by heating the juice of ½ a fresh lemon, an equal amount of water, a lump of butter, and honey to sweeten. Drink it hot and stay in bed afterward. It will make you perspire.

When you have a cold or feel one coming on, try grapefruit power:

Wash a grapefruit, cut it in ½, and squeeze the juice into a glass. Cut the rind in small pieces and boil slowly for 1 hour on low heat in 4 glasses of water. Strain off the pulp and discard. Add the juice to this hot liquid. This should make 3 glasses. Drink 1 glass hot at once, the second in another hour, and the last in two hours, hot or cool.

If needed, this can be repeated each day until the cold is broken.

To relieve a stuffed-up nose and make colds go away faster:

Mix 1 level teaspoon salt with 1 pint distilled water, and add a couple of drops of eau de Cologne for the pleasant smell if preferred. If you don't have distilled water, let tap water stand overnight in shallow containers to let all the chlorine evaporate. Snuff some up your nose or use a spray device about every four hours.

COUGHS

HONEY SYRUP

From New England comes the following recipe for cough syrup:

Ingredients

  1 lemon
  2 tablespoons glycerine
  ¾ cup honey

Boil the whole lemon slowly, covering with water. Next, cut the lemon in ½ and extract all the juice. Stir in 2 tablespoons of glycerine and add honey, mixing well. Take the cough syrup 1 teaspoon at a time according to need, stirring well before each dose.

If a cough prevents you from sleeping, keep a teaspoon and some honey by your bed. When you feel a cough coming on, suck on some honey and the desire to cough disappears like magic.

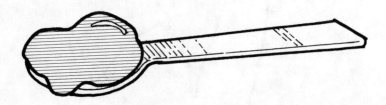

SUNFLOWER SYRUP

While chest coughs and congestion are hardly agreeable, this remedy is truly delightful. Boil ½ cup (2 ounces) sunflower seeds in 5 cups water until water is reduced to approximately 2 cups. Strain, and stir in ¾ cup gin and ½ cup sugar, mixing well. Take 1 to 2 teaspoons four times a day.

ONION SYRUP

Onion-based cough syrups are traditional folk remedies around the world. Here's a sampling.

From Sweden:

>1 cup honey
>1 cup water
>½ cup chopped onion
>⅓ cup pine-tree buds

Mix honey and water well and then add other ingredients. Bring to a boil. Reduce heat and simmer covered for twenty minutes. Adults can take a dosage of 1 tablespoon; children, 1 to 2 teaspoons as needed.

From England:

    6 medium-sized onions
    ½ cup honey

Peel and finely chop the onions and put them in a double boiler with the honey. Cover. Simmer gently for two hours, then strain. Take 1 tablespoon of the warm syrup as needed.

From Mexico:

    1 tablespoon flaxseed
    3 cups water
    ⅔ cup finely chopped onion
    ½ cup honey
    ¼ cup lemon juice

Mix flaxseed and water in a pot and simmer until the liquid is reduced to half. Remove from heat, stir in honey and onion, then cool. Add lemon juice and take 1 tablespoon as needed.

PHLEGM REMOVAL

Gently massage your throat, then drink warm water with some baking soda mixed in. Make yourself cough to loosen phlegm.

CYSTITIS

For urinary infections, stop drinking coffee and alcohol and start drinking lots of cranberry juice. Cranberry juice contains benzoic acid, a natural preservative that inhibits the growth of bacteria. The acid environment is harmful to the bacteria. Cranberry juice also contains vitamin C, and drinking a lot of liquid flushes the entire system.

EARS

EARACHE

An old country remedy calls for mixing a handful of coarse salt with a handful of bran, tying this into a muslin bag. Slowly heat it in the oven at a low temperature and when warm—not hot—to the touch, apply to the sore ear.

Another treatment for a simple earache is to pour a little olive oil into a teaspoon and warm it with a match or candle. Test it against the back of your hand to see that it is warm, not hot. Lie down with the bad ear up and pour in the warm drops. To hold in the warmth, hold a hot-water bottle wrapped in a towel against the ear. If the earache doesn't go away, a doctor should be consulted.

EAR WAX

For accumulated ear wax, mix 3 drops of any liquid dishwashing detergent into 1 teaspoon warm water. Pour ½ this mixture into each ear, lying first on one side and then the other, using a towel to catch any liquid that runs out. Do this three times a day for three days. If the wax isn't gone by this time, flush the ear gently with warm water, using an all-rubber ear syringe.

Peroxide is also used for the same purpose.

EYES

SOMETHING IN YOUR EYE?

Pull open the upper eyelid and with your other hand blow your nose three times. It sounds strange but it stimulates tears.

TIRED EYES

If your eyes feel tired or strained, wring out a washcloth in cold water and lie on your back with the cloth over your eyes. Refold the cloth periodically to put the cold next to your eyes.

Another suggestion for tired eyes:

Put slices of cucumbers or wet, used tea-bags on your eyes.

Eye-palm position to rest the eyes:

Rub the palms of your hands together briskly, creating some heat. Hold them over your eyes for about half a minute, as shown in the drawing. Repeat two or three times.

Don't write with red ink for long periods of time. Studies have shown that red, perhaps because it is an unconscious signal of alarm, can cause headache and eyestrain.

Eyestrain can make you feel tired to a much greater extent than you think. If you are doing close eyework, periodically stop and do this exercise:

Hold a forefinger pointing upward about 10 inches in front of your nose. Look at the finger, then look at the end of the room beyond the finger, and alternate.

iⅼⅼⅼ

SENSITIVITY TO LIGHT

Does it hurt your eyes to move from indoors to bright sunlight? Do this exercise and throw away your sunglasses:

Sit or stand comfortably facing the sun or a light bulb (about 18 inches from a light bulb). Close the eyelids and slowly, smoothly, turn the head from side to side as though saying no. It should get much darker at the two sides and be quite bright in the center of each swing of the head. Do this for three to five minutes, twice a day, following it with the eye-palm position (see page 29).

iⅼⅼⅼ

BLACK EYE

The witch hazel cure for a black eye couldn't be easier. Soak a bandage in extract of witch hazel and bind it over the closed eye. Keep the bandage moist and if possible lie down, keeping your feet slightly raised.

BAGS UNDER THE EYES

An actress tells us she drinks no liquids for about twenty hours before she is going to be photographed. Liquid, she says, goes straight to the eyes and makes them look puffy, as does salt.

A model friend of ours uses Preparation H under her eyes whenever they look baggy. The effects are temporary, but it looks great for an evening on the town. The same remedy is known in California as the "grandmother's facelift."

Try putting some grated raw potato under the eyes for ten to fifteen minutes at a time.

BEFORE

AFTER

STIES

Sties are annoying, but they go away by themselves. This remedy hurries their healing:

Fold a washcloth in four and dip it in water as hot as possible without being uncomfortable. Wring it partially dry and hold it on the eye for twenty minutes, keeping the cloth hot.

EYELASHES

Vaseline on eyelashes make them grow thicker and longer. Even if it doesn't, it makes them *look* that way.

Some people recommend castor oil instead.

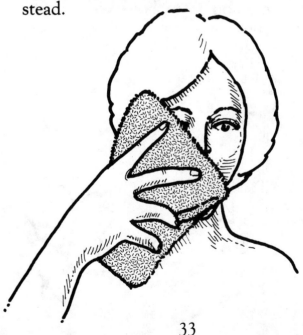

FAINTNESS

Have the person who feels faint sit down and put his head down, below the level of the heart. Blood goes to the brain, and the person should feel better in five or ten minutes.

From overheating and faintness—for example, on a hot summer day:

Hold ice cubes against the inside of your wrist. All the blood in your body circulates through your wrist within minutes, and relief is immediate.

Another method is to hold your wrists under cold running water.

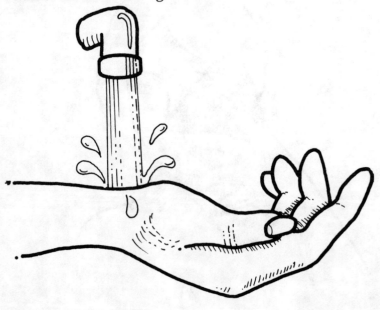

FEET

BLISTERS

An expert on footwear for athletes shares this advice:

If you get a blister on the foot, put Vaseline on it but no Band-Aid. (The blister will only rub against the Band-Aid if you use one, and rubbing is what caused it in the first place.) The Vaseline makes anything that comes into contact with it slide instead of rub.

Soothe and hasten the healing of blisters on the feet by rubbing them with fresh-cut grass.

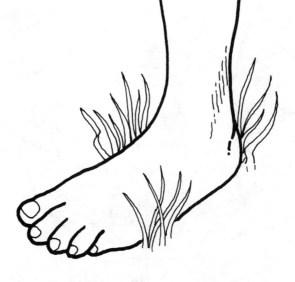

CALLUSES

Take every opportunity to walk barefoot in the sand. There isn't anything in the world better for your feet. It exercises them, it is good for the arches, and the action of the sand on the skin helps slough off dead skin and calluses.

TIRED FEET

Soak tired feet in lukewarm water to which a cup of vinegar has been added.

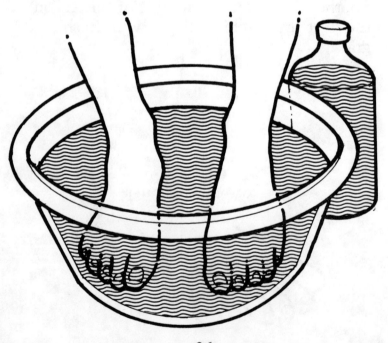

FEVER

A brew for fever or sore throat:

Put into a small pan 2 aspirins, 1 level teaspoon salt, juice of ½ fresh lemon, 3 tablespoons white rum, 1 teaspoon honey. Cook, stirring, and drink hot. Go to bed afterward.

Fever reducer:

1½ teaspoons cream of tartar
½ teaspoon lemon juice
1 pint warm water
½ teaspoon honey to taste

Combine all the ingredients and drink a glassful to relieve fever from sunburn and other mild burns.

To bring down a fever:

Take 3 cooking apples, core, and slice. Place them in a saucepan, add 3¾ cups water and bring to a boil. Then simmer until the apples begin to break apart. Remove from heat and strain off the liquid without pressing the apple mixture. Mix 2 tablespoons honey with the juice, chill, and drink as needed.

GOUT

Gout sufferers:

Eat a whole bowl of cherries the first day of an attack, and 6 to 8 cherries per day every day thereafter. It doesn't matter whether the cherries are fresh, canned, or frozen.

HAIR

HAIR LIGHTENER

Put lemon juice on your hair and go out into the sun. After washing, the hair will be lighter and shinier. Avoid getting lemon or lime juice on the skin, however, since these can cause a bad burn when exposed to the sun.

Follow your shampoo with a rinse of camomile tea to lighten hair.

BEER SHAMPOO

Many beauticians feel that manufactured shampoos are too soapy for hair. This beer shampoo both cuts the shampoo of your choice and builds body:

Take a cup of beer and boil until it is reduced to ¼ cup, add to your favorite shampoo, and use. The remainder of the beer can be used as a setting lotion.

HERBAL SHAMPOOS

Make up the basic recipe for shampoo with herbs selected for your particular needs.

Basic Recipe:

> 1 oz. castile soap
> 8 oz. water
> 1 ounce herb mixture

To make, simmer herbs in water for twenty minutes, then strain. Stir in liquid castile soap and add a couple of drops of your favorite essential oil.

For oily hair:

Mix equal parts peppermint, spearmint, quassia chips, lemon grass, witch hazel bark, white oak bark, nettle, willow bark, sage, orange peel, raspberry leaf, and strawberry leaf. (If you can't find all the ingredients, make it up with what's available.)

For dry hair:

Acacia flowers, elder flowers, comfrey leaf and root, rosemary, orange flowers, and camomile.

For problem scalp, dandruff, and itchy scalp:

Witch hazel bark, white oak bark, yarrow, artichoke leaves, nettle, and willow bark.

DRY SHAMPOO

Here is a fine dry shampoo originating in the British Isles:

Mix together 2 ounces cornmeal with 1 ounce powdered orris root and sprinkle well into the hair. Gently massage scalp. Brush until all traces of the powder are gone.

HAIR CONDITIONERS

A few drops of rosemary or lavender oil brushed or massaged into the hair each day makes a wonderful hair conditioner. Those with dry hair will probably prefer the lavender oil.

For greasy hair, rinse with diluted lemon juice or with a brew made from boiled, strained nettles.

Simmer together 1 cup olive oil and a herbal mixture of horsetail, rosemary, sage, and comfrey that equals a total of ¼ cup. Strain, then add 25,000 I.U. vitamin E oil and two drops pure lavender oil. Use a few drops a day either massaged or brushed into hair.

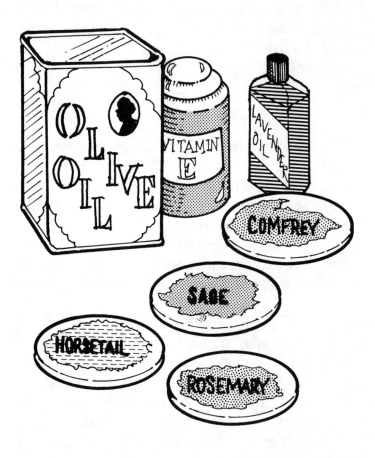

DANDRUFF

Dandruff can be cured and lifeless and difficult-to-handle hair brought into line if you take a tablespoon of corn oil internally at breakfast time and another at night.

Corn oil can also serve the same purpose when warmed and massaged into the scalp. Then wrap a warm moist towel around your head. Repeat the towel application six times and shampoo. Dandruff will be banished and hair will shine.

ITCHING SCALP

Mix 1 teaspoon of apple cider vinegar to 1 cup of water. Dip in comb before using and comb hair until it is well saturated. This treatment will return your scalp to its normal acid balance and relieve the itching. However, it may straighten a permanent, so you may want to consider an alternative solution if you've given your hair a curlier touch.

For dry hair or an itchy scalp, massage a couple of raw eggs into the scalp. Care must be taken to wash this out with warm and not hot water, however, or the smell of cooked egg will stay on your head for a while. Follow with a rinse of 1 teaspoon white vinegar in 1 quart warm water.

MISCELLANEOUS HAIR TIPS

Don't clean your hairbrush at the same time you clean your hair. If you brush your hair with a somewhat dirty hairbrush, you are putting your own natural hair oils back into your hair.

For static in your hair, spray on some Zero-Stat from the record cabinet or some Static Guard from the laundry supplies.

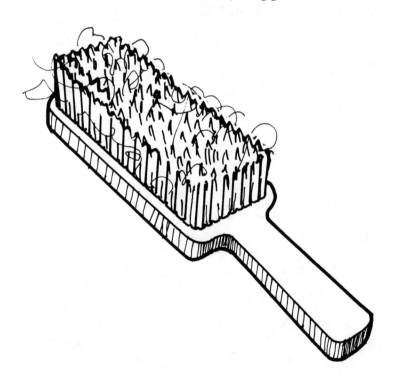

HANDS

HAND CARE

Hands get an unbelievable amount of use over a lifetime, and it is well worth taking care of them. Here are some ways.

Use a lot of hand lotion or Vaseline on the hands before doing work such as gardening or painting. It will make paint and dirt removal much easier afterward.

Dig fingernails into a bar of soap before gardening or other dirty work, to ease cleaning them later.

The *Harvard Medical School Newsletter* says that Dove soap is the bath and hand soap that is among the easiest on the skin.

Dairymaid's lotion:
Chapped hands can be gently relieved with this easy-to-make lotion.

Mix 1 slice lemon with ½ cup milk. Let stand for two to three hours or until the milk is slightly curdled. Remove the lemon, refrigerate the lotion, and use as needed.

Dip fingers in ice water to make nail polish dry quickly.

HANGNAILS AND BROKEN FINGERNAILS

If you are subject to hangnails and broken fingernails, use the trick that professional guitarists use:

Massage your fingernails, including the cuticles. The improved blood circulation does the rest.

SMELLS AND STAINS

Get strong smells off fingers by using lemon peel or juice, a slice of raw potato, or a paste made of dry mustard. The lemon will also remove stains caused by the preparation of vegetables and other kitchen work.

To remove the odor of gasoline from your hands, rub them with salt.

To get inkstains off your fingers, rub with a wet unburned match.

Grandmother's trick for whitening hands:

Rub a squeezed lemon over your hands after washing them with soap and water.

HANGOVERS

After a night of heavy drinking, take an aspirin and a couple of glasses of water before going to sleep. The water helps the dehydration that drinking can cause, and the aspirin counters the tendency of alcohol to constrict blood flow.

Vitamin B with a couple glasses of water is also recommended.

Eat pizza the day after. The grease helps.

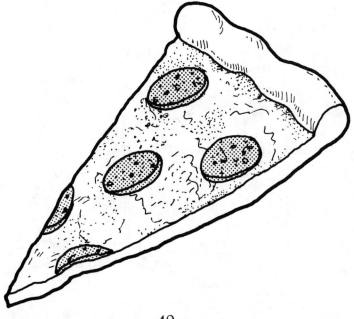

HAY FEVER

From New England comes this cure for hay fever:

It would be ideal to eat honey made from the pollen of the plant you are allergic to (as a form of immunization). But if you can't arrange that, chew honeycomb during the hay fever season and take a tablespoon of apple cider vinegar every three hours or as symptoms reappear.

Orange peel candy—delicious, and it relieves hay fever too!

Cut orange peels into small strips and soak in apple cider vinegar for several hours. Drain well and cook in a pan with honey. Refrigerate and eat as hay fever symptoms appear.

The following will reduce the symptoms of hay fever:

Mix 1 heaping teaspoon salt with a pint of warm water, making certain that all the salt is thoroughly dissolved. Gargle with this solution and then gently blow the nose clear of all mucus. Next, snuff salt water solution up the nose, one nostril at a time.

HEADACHE

HEADACHE CURE

Heat equal amounts of apple cider vinegar and water, then inhale the steam. If headache returns, repeat.

Got a headache? You probably have these ingredients for a cure handy. Take two aspirins and a cup of coffee. The aspirin will relieve the pain while the caffeine constricts swollen, throbbing blood vessels.

A large mint leaf, rolled and stuck partway into the nostril, is a good method for getting rid of a headache.

For a headache, put a large dab of Vicks VapoRub on your forehead.

MIGRAINE

Migraine sufferers can try inhaling from a jar containing strong mustard. The sulphur fumes are what helps.

Sufferers of migraine headaches will probably agree that any remedy that prevents the headache is most welcome. From New England comes a tasty cure:

Take 2 teaspoons of honey with each meal to prevent migraines. And should you get a headache anyway, take another tablespoon immediately. Drink lots of water when taking honey.

HICCUPS

Sometimes an attack of hiccups seems impossible to cure. However, this country remedy has been around for a long time because it works for many people. It's also quick and tasty. Take a lump of sugar that has been thoroughly saturated with lemon juice and let it slowly dissolve in your mouth. If necessary, repeat the dose.

Some more hiccups remedies, each raved about by its practitioners:

Cover your head with or breathe into a paper bag. The carbon dioxide in your breath has a calming effect on the hiccup-producing mechanism of your body.

This next one is very tricky and will take practice. Stand with your legs about 2 feet apart and lean forward at the hips. Your eyes will be looking right at your knees. In this position, drink a glass of cold water. If you can *do* it, it will stop the hiccups.

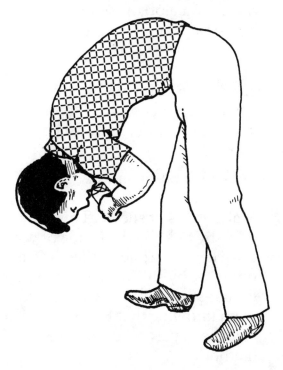

Other cures for hiccups:

Try to touch your elbows in back of you.

Exhale slowly and completely; hold as long as possible.

Eat 1 tablespoon of honey.

Swallow 7 times without hiccuping.

Give the tongue a sharp yank.

Drink a glass of ice water.

Put a cold compress on the back of the neck.

Swallow a glob of sour cream.

Take 9 sips of water on one breath.

A tendency toward severe hiccups seems to run in families. These two remedies are considered fail-safe by one such hiccup-prone family:

Suck on a bit of lemon.

Make yourself sneeze. This can be done by tickling the inside of your nostril with a tissue rolled into a point, or by sniffing some red pepper. Perhaps you will derive some comfort from knowing that Plato is alleged to have been partial to the sneeze method.

MENSTRUATION

MENSTRUAL CRAMPS

Lower salt intake for a week before your menstrual period, to reduce cramps and bloating.

Take slightly warmed vodka or gin for menstrual cramps.

Menstrual cramps, digestive upsets, calming a nervous stomach—catnip tea:
Use 2 teaspoons of the dried herb to each cup of boiling water. Let steep covered for five to ten minutes in order to reach desired strength. Sweeten with honey, or add milk or lemon to taste.

MENSTRUAL FLOW

If unusually heavy menstrual flow is a problem, drink yarrow tea as soon as bleeding starts. Start with a teaspoon of yarrow to each cup of boiling water, let steep for five to ten minutes, and drink. If necessary, tea can be made stronger, using up to 2 teaspoons of yarrow for each cup of water. Drink several cups a day.

NOSEBLEEDS

Stop nosebleds by sitting quietly and pinching the nose firmly for ten minutes, or until bleeding has fully stopped. If that doesn't work, wet a piece of cotton with hydrogen peroxide or Vaseline and pack the nostril with the cotton, leaving part of it outside the nose. The cotton should be left inside for several hours and removed with care.

Some people suffer from chronic nosebleeds. This can be alleviated by rubbing a little Vaseline inside the nostrils twice daily. Oranges, tomatoes, and other fruits may also help to strengthen the blood vessels, which in turn will help prevent nosebleeds.

To stop a nosebleed, tie a string tightly under the fingernail of the pinky finger on the hand opposite the nostril that is bleeding.

Jamaican remedy

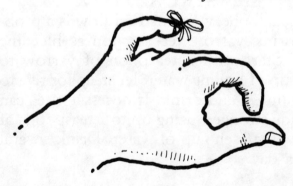

SKIN PROBLEMS

TO REMOVE BANDAGES

Get adhesive tape and bandages off painlessly by saturating them with vegetable oil
before removal.

BOILS

Bread poultice:

To draw the poisons in boils and other
minor infections, make a bread poultice.
Cover 6 slices of bread with water and boil
until mushy. Then wrap some of the bread in
a piece of clean flannel cloth and apply to
boil. When cool, remove and replace with
another application. This may need to be
done several times to be effective. It is a
remedy that has been used with success for
many, many years in Ireland.

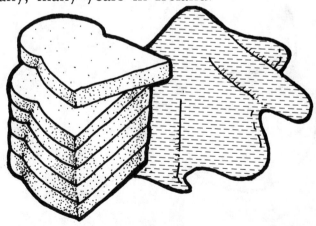

For boils, carbuncles, and other swellings, mix equal parts honey and flour and apply. The mixture will draw out the waste material painlessly and quickly.

BRUISES

Bruise easily? Try eating more oranges and grapefruits, including the white pulp. In addition to the vitamin C, the pulp contains bioflavonoids, which strengthen the capillaries whose rupture causes the black-and-blue marks.

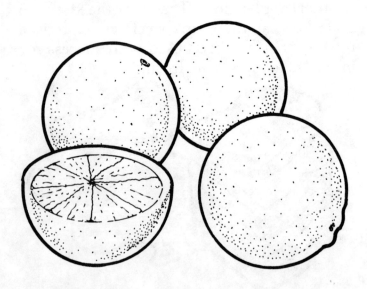

BURNS

For burns, apply cold water or ice instantly. *Do not use butter or grease.* If no cold water is available, press anything cold against the burn, such as metal.

From Poland comes the advice to follow the cold application with a sprinkling of salt.

From Germany the advice is to follow with a sprinkling of flour.

If you burn yourself and blisters form, don't break the blisters. Put a clean bandage or gauze on it, then cover the whole thing with a plastic bag. Air makes a burn hurt more.

Vitamin E herbal oil:

This remedy for burns comes from Germany. Place ½ cup wheat germ oil and ½ cup honey in a blender and mix at low speed until well blended. Add enough comfrey leaves to make a thick paste and blend at medium speed to a smooth mixture. Store oil in refrigerator and use as needed on burns.

Burned (including sunburned), irritated, or itchy skin can be relieved with wet tea bags or cold tea compresses. The tannic acid in the tea has a calming and healing effect.

To relieve sunburn:

> Apply cider vinegar, or
> pat with a wet teabag, or
> apply a paste of baking soda and water, or
> take a bath with baking soda mixed into the water.

COLD SORES

Apply hydrogen peroxide. It is also good for sterilizing cuts.

Dab a cold sore with whiskey:
 Dip your finger into the liquor and rub the sore lightly.

CUTS

Smear honey on a cut or bruise and cover with a bandage for faster healing. Add more honey when it disappears from the bandage.

Cuts from coral and sea urchins can be dangerous. Wash with ½ a lemon or lime to prevent infection.

If you can't get to your first-aid supplies, tear off a piece of brown-paper bag and put it on a cut. The paper will soak up the blood and act as a kind of bandage, protecting the wound.

DEODORANT
Low-cost deodorant:
   Wash with baking soda for an inexpensive and nonirritating alternative to using deodorants.

FRECKLES
Freckle banish:
   Lightly oil the skin with almond oil. Then combine 6 tablespoons of buttermilk with 1 teaspoon of freshly grated horseradish. Apply to oiled skin. Leave on for twenty minutes, then remove with warm water. If used on the face, moisturize after rinsing.

To bleach a yellowed, faded tan, apply buttermilk several times a day, each time letting it dry and then rinsing with lukewarm water.

Our Victorian ancestors had some sound home remedies. For brown (liver) spots, unwanted freckles, or a fading tan that you no longer want, rub in some lemon juice at night and in the morning. Repeat for three to four weeks. Castor oil will do the same thing.

IRRITATIONS

The aloe vera cactus is one of nature's wonder plants. Keep one growing on your windowsill, and when you have a cut, burn, or a poison ivy rash, mosquito bite, or pimple, slice off the end of one of the arms of the plant and apply the sap to the affected area. The plant will heal itself in a matter of days, and so will you.

ITCHING

To relieve the itching caused by poison ivy, oak, and sumac, pediatricians recommend applying Ban Roll-On to the itchy area. Reapply whenever it feels itchy again.

An eminent pediatrician advises spraying chicken pox with ordinary spray starch to relieve itching.

For any fungus infection anywhere in the body, eat lots of yogurt.

If taking antibiotics, eat yogurt to replace the body's natural bacteria killed by the medicine.

PIMPLES

Dip a Q-tip in a lemon or in alcohol and apply to a pimple. It will dry it up faster.

Pimples can be cured by mixing a teaspoon of alum to a quart of water and washing with this solution three times a day.

Apply a slice of tomato to a pimple and leave it on the skin for a half hour. The tomato slice can be held on with an adhesive bandage.

From a frugal and beautiful Frenchwoman comes this advice:

Crush oatmeal into a powder. Mix it with a little water to form a paste, and apply to pimples or oily skin or rashes. It soothes as well as heals.

⁂

Blackheads, pimples, and other minor skin eruptions are said to be cured by this old-time remedy:

Drink a strong tea made of red-clover blossoms instead of drinking water. The tea is made by boiling 3 to 4 tablespoons of granulated red clover to each quart of water for a half hour.

FOR SHINGLES

A paste made of baking soda and water.

SPLINTERS

Wonder cure for splinters that don't easily come out:

Sprinkle salt on the skin, then put a slice of tomato against it. Keep the tomato on overnight (use adhesive tape, gauze and a plastic bag to keep the bed clean) and the splinter will come out easily the next morning. For fingers and toes, you might use half a cherry tomato.

Small splinters can be removed by nearly filling a wide-mouthed bottle with hot water and placing the injured part over the mouth of the bottle. Press firmly. The suction will push the flesh down and the steam will extract the splinter. This should work in just one or two minutes. If not, it should be easy to press the splinter out, since the skin will be softened.

Ice makes a fine anesthetic. Use it to numb the taste buds before taking unpleasant-tasting medicine, or to numb the skin before removing a hard-to-get-at splinter.

WARTS

To remove warts:

> Cut a potato in half and throw half away.
> Rub remaining half on wart.
> Bury the half potato by the light of a full moon.
> The wart will disappear by the next full moon.

Believe it or not, this remedy has worked on several people I know after the doctors' other methods failed.

Another remedy is to tape a slice of garlic clove on the wart. Change the garlic three times a day; continue for a week.

SKIN CARE

DRY SKIN

Vaseline is as effective as any lip gloss and lip moisturizer combined. It can go on top of lipstick; to get a sharp outline use a brush.

To tone and moisturize the face:

Clean your face thoroughly, then wet with water. Put Vaseline on your fingertips and gently massage both the Vaseline and the water into the face, using small circular motions.

Moisturizing eye cream and dry spot care-taker that's easy enough to make:

Mix 3 ounces of lanolin with just enough almond oil to make a consistency similar to that of cold cream. Add a few drops of your favorite essential oil, place in a jar with cap, and use as needed.

Hand and body lotion:

> 3 ounces almond oil
> 1 ounce lanolin
> 1 ounce aloe vera gel
> 1 ounce rosewater

Melt oils together, remove from heat, beat in aloe vera and rosewater. It couldn't be much easier!

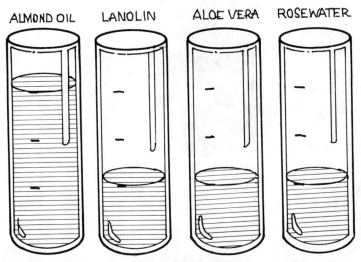

ALMOND OIL   LANOLIN   ALOE VERA   ROSEWATER

Orange mint face cream:

Melt together 5 ounces lanolin and 3 ounces almond oil, and remove from heat. Beat in 3 ounces orange flower water and 1 ounce of strong mint tea until creamy.

You've heard of food for thought; well, this is food for the skin. Melt together 1 part lanolin and 1 part coconut oil. Remove from heat and beat in 1 part aloe vera gel and vitamin E oil using 10,000 I.U. per cup of lotion.

Rosewater and glycerin have long been used as a skin softener. In fact, in colonial times it was the basic toiletry in every woman's cosmetic chest:

Mix 3 ounces glycerin with 7 ounces rosewater, bottle, and it's ready for use. For variety you can use other available scented waters in place of the rosewater. The proportions remain the same.

Face cream:

Melt together 2 tablespoons lanolin, 2 tablespoons coconut oil, and 2 tablespoons apricot kernel oil. Remove from heat and beat in 3 tablespoons rosewater or orange flower water until creamy.

Use moisturizer as soon as you finish bathing—it locks in the moisture that your skin has just absorbed in the water.

Put baby oil and soapy lather on your legs before shaving them. It keeps them soft and minimizes nicks.

OILY SKIN

Witch hazel makes a great astringent, but it smells a bit, so you might like to add a little rosewater or other scent.

llli

Gypsy astringent:

Make up an herb formula of 1 part each of roses, lavender, rosemary, sage, orange peel, and lemon peel, and then add 2 parts mint. To every 2 ounces of the herb formula add 1 pint of apple cider vinegar, and place in a glass jar with a good lid. Allow to sit for two weeks, then strain. Add 1 cup rosewater to each pint and use. This recipe is reputed to be the first herbal product ever sold in Europe and comes from a Hungarian gypsy recipe.

FACIALS

Oatmeal scrub:

This recipe has many an expensive store-bought duplicate. You can make it yourself at a fraction of the cost. Mix together:

> 1 egg white, whipped
> coarse oatmeal
> 1 teaspoon honey
> rosewater (optional, for fragrance)

It makes a cleansing, invigorating scrub. If almond oil is added, it is also good for the rough skin on the elbows.

To clean pores, sprinkle salt onto a damp washcloth and gently rub.

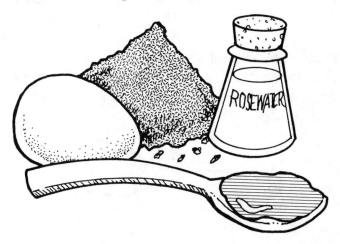

To open and clean pores, unclog sinuses, and improve skin, bring a small pot of water to a boil, adding a handful of camomile, rosemary, or thyme. Simmer about five minutes. With your skin clean and your hair pulled back, put the pot on a table and sit, relaxed, with a towel making a tent so the steam is directed to the face. It should be hot, bringing blood to the skin, but it should not burn. Enjoy for a maximum of fifteen minutes.

Follow with a cold water rinse, a mask, or a scrub.

A mushroom brush (inexpensive and available in department stores or gourmet shops) makes a fine facial scrubber. Designed to brush dirt off mushrooms without wetting them or damaging the surface and small enough to carry in your makeup kit, it is an excellent device for sloughing dried or flaked skin from your face. Used with slightly more pressure, it also works well on elbows, shins, and ankles.

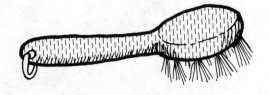

Cucumbers have long been used in beauty preparations, and although various concoctions are flourishing today, they are based on recipes of old. This one is from the turn of the century—the early nineteenth century, that is.

Cucumber facial and dry skin balm:

>   4 cucumbers
>   ½ cup rosewater
>   ½ teaspoon tincture of benzoin

Blend or grate the cucumbers, place them in a linen towel, and squeeze out as much juice as possible. Add rosewater and benzoin and mix well. It is very important to store this in the refrigerator as it has a tendency to spoil quickly. Use as a facial rinse or on raw chapped skin.

The best facial mask is plain old egg white. To get rid of blackheads, refine pores, and tighten skin, apply the egg white to a clean face and let it dry. Leave it on for fifteen minutes or more, then wash off with warm water.

If you are willing to take slightly more trouble, the honey variation feels quite luxurious. Beat 1 egg white until very stiff, add 1 tablespoon honey, and beat again until the mixture is a very thick whipped cream. Spread on the face for fifteen minutes and wash off with warm water.

Avocado-honey facial:

Most medicines combine a number of ingredients, on the theory that each person reacts slightly differently and that a combination is more likely to benefit the largest number of people. In line with this theory, you might like to try the avocado-honey facial. Combine 1 whole egg, 1 tablespoon mashed avocado, 2 tablespoons honey and whip together until smooth. Again, leave on face for fifteen minutes and rinse.

WRINKLES

From the French Riviera comes this rich recipe for "tired skin":

Mix the yolk of 1 egg with ½ teaspoon lemon juice and ½ teaspoon olive oil. Apply to face, wait fifteen minutes, wash off with warm water. Pat dry.

Rub a slice of cucumber on your skin to tighten and soften it.

The Crisco way to wrinkle-free skin:
Apply Crisco oil to face and neck, then gently massage it in with the back of a spoon. Use a demitasse spoon for around the eyes, a soup ladle for neck and chin, and a teaspoon for the other areas. In addition, drink lots of water to increase the moisture in the body.

Farm-fresh wrinkle remover:
Mix together 2 tablespoons fresh cream with 1 teaspoon honey and apply it to the face. Let it dry. Remove by washing gently with warm water.

Wrinkle chaser:

Cool and refreshing, this wonderfully rich cream is one of the basic natural cosmetics.

Separate one egg. Put the yolk in a small jar that has a tight-fitting cover. Add 2 tablespoons honey to the yolk and stir very well until thick and creamy. Add the egg white, put cover on tightly, and shake very hard.

These additions will make this cream more pleasant and easier to use:

Add a few drops of your favorite scent for the sheer pleasure of it and a few drops of benzoin to keep it from spoiling. Keep refrigerated and use nightly on face and neck.

For smoother skin:
Ingredients

> ½ ounce cocoa butter
> 1 ounce almond oil
> 1 ounce palm oil
> 1 ounce persic oil
> 1 ounce olive oil
> ¼ teaspoon tincture of benzoin
> a few drops of your favorite essence
> a capped bottle

Melt together first five ingredients in a double boiler. Remove from heat, add benzoin and a few drops of your choice of essential oil, pour into bottle, and it's ready to use!

Firm the throat muscles under the chin that give away age more than any other muscles by doing "the gargoyle," an ancient yogic practice. This exercise can be done while driving the car, sitting in a dark movie theater, watching TV, or whenever. Stick your tongue out and down as far as it will go. You will see improvement within days.

SORE THROAT

SORE THROAT REMEDIES

Singers use this remedy for sore throats:

Put Vaseline on your neck, particularly on the throat. Cover it by tying a handkerchief around your neck. In the morning the sore throat will be either gone or very much better.

Sore throat remedy:
Chew on licorice root, or boil some in water to make a tea.

⚜

GARGLING

Hasten the departure of a sore throat by gargling every two hours with warm water into which salt and a little baking soda have been mixed.

⚜

Another gargle for a sore throat and chest congestion was originally recommended to us by a pharmacist:
Stir 2 tablespoons of apple cider vinegar (don't use another kind of vinegar) into a glass of hot water and gargle every few hours until well. It works beautifully.

⚜

For the relief of a sore throat or as a refreshing mouthwash, try this honey gargle made from an old Egyptian recipe:
Make 1 cup of sage tea, add 2 tablespoons honey, and stir. Next add 1 cup vinegar, 1 teaspoon oil of sweet almonds, and 5 drops oil of cloves. Stir all ingredients together and bottle for use as needed.

SORE MUSCLES

LINIMENTS

Beat up a liniment to relieve the pain of sore muscles. Take 1 tablespoon turpentine and 1 tablespoon apple cider vinegar and beat together with 1 egg yolk. Rub well into the skin around the sensitive area.

Another powerful liniment, one that doesn't smell of turpentine, is made by gently boiling 1 tablespoon of cayenne pepper in 1 pint of cider vinegar. Bottle the liquid while it is hot.

MASSAGE

Wish you had someone to massage the back of your neck and shoulder muscles, but there is no one available? Try this:

Hunch your shoulders straight up as far as they go. Now roll your head to one side until one ear touches a shoulder, and roll the head backwards and around slowly until the other ear touches the other shoulder.

NATURAL REMEDY

Here is a natural remedy for all kinds of stiffness in the body:

Chop 1 grapefruit, 2 oranges, and 3 lemons, with their skins. Put in a blender with 1 teaspoon cream of tartar. Add an equal amount of water and drink 2 tablespoons twice a day.

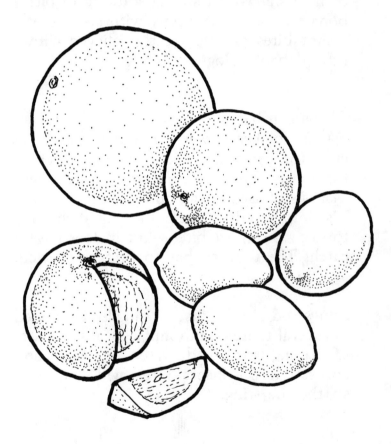

STINGS, BITES, INSECT REPELLENTS

STINGS AND BITES

Bee or wasp stings can be soothed by rubbing a little lemon juice over the sting. If it looks particularly red and swollen, make a poultice of lime water or a strong solution of bicarbonate of soda and apply with a soft cloth.

Ant bites can be greatly relieved with a little dab of cologne.

Chewin' tobacco plug:

Our forebears were a hardy lot. This cure for removing the sting and swelling from insect bites is an old frontier treatment that is still used in agricultural communities. It's simple to do—just put a plug of chewing tobacco on insect bites—but it does have a catch! The tobacco has to first be chewed.

Stings and bites of insects can also be treated in several more commonplace ways. A paste of baking soda and water or water and cornstarch on insect bites will cool and soothe the sting.

Another treatment for insect bites and allergy rashes:

Apply a paste made of Ac'cent (monosodium glutamate) and water.

A dab of toothpaste on a mosquito bite takes away the sting.

Apply clear ammonia to a bee sting to take away the pain.

To relieve the itching of red-ant bites, apply a weak solution of clear household ammonia.

Paint the skin where a chigger has bitten with clear nail polish. This will kill the chigger by cutting off its oxygen supply.

At the beach, use vodka for jellyfish stings.

INSECT REPELLENTS

Put a stick of incense or its odorless equivalent, punk, into the ground where you are sitting to keep mosquitoes away.

A pot of geraniums will keep mosquitoes away.

Have you noticed how some people get all the mosquito bites while others in the same group get none? Two possible explanations for this unfairness have come to light. Mosquitoes will zoom for the people with the highest body temperatures and will stay away from those with a high amount of thiamine in their systems. Before your next camping trip, try eating large amounts of thiamine, or vitamin B_1, found in Brewer's yeast, Brazil nuts, sunflower seeds, and fish.

Pennyroyal oil rubbed into the skin keeps many biting insects away. The strong smell may also keep people away, so use sparingly or combine with perfume.

Some bruised elder leaves in a saucer repel flies and other insects.

Carbolic soap rubbed around the ankles discourages ticks.

American lore of old holds that spreading camomile flowers about the house will rid it of fleas.

Moth repellent:

Camphor works very well, but doesn't do much for the smell of your clothes. However, making little cloth bags and filling them with a handful each of rosemary, pennyroyal, and vetiver, plus six bay leaves, will do the job and leave a pleasant odor.

Another sachet for people tired of the smell of mothballs contains 1 ounce each of lavender flowers, lemon peel, cassia, and powdered cloves. Put the mixture in little bags and use in drawers and closets. It will do the same work as mothballs.

French insect repellent oil:

Simmer sesame seed or safflower oil with either feverfew blossoms or dried feverfew for twenty minutes. Remove from heat and let cool. Then add 8 finely chopped garlic cloves, pour into a bottle, and let stand for a week. During that time, shake bottle occasionally. Strain and *voilà!* it's ready to use. The oil can be applied directly to the skin as an insect repellent or can be used as a remedy for bites . . . if you forget to use it in advance.

Roaches:

Here's a remedy that roaches probably have not yet adapted to. Mix equal amounts of oil of peppermint or spearmint and oil of pennyroyal and apply around baseboards, kitchen cabinets, and other likely spots. Boric acid can also be used for the same purpose (unless you have pets or babies around the house to whom this would be poisonous).

STOMACH UPSET

ACID INDIGESTION

For acid indigestion after a big meal, eat an apple. It contains pepsin, an enzyme that helps break down food in the stomach.

To cut the acid in coffee, sprinkle a little salt among the grounds before the water goes through them.

STOMACHACHE

For a stomachache, stir ¼ teaspoon bicarbonate of soda into a glass of water and drink. It will settle a stomach that is only mildly upset; for a more severe upset, it will make one throw up, and then feel better.

An old Arabic remedy advises 1 or 2 teaspoons of straight rosewater for a stomachache.

For an upset stomach, drink club soda or any of the cola drinks. (This is also good for infants.)

The French advise a small glass of anisette, either straight or on the rocks, for mild stomach upset.

For a stomachache:

Hold the webbed skin between your thumb and forefinger with the thumb and forefinger of the other hand. Massage the slightly meaty part, just beyond the very loose webbing, gently but firmly. Do this for a minute, then switch and do the other hand. If one hand hurts more than the other, massage the tender one longer.

CAR SICKNESS

Car sickness troubles many people. Try beating the white of an egg with the juice of a lemon and sweetening slightly. Drink just before your next long car ride for relief from nausea.

For a laxative, take equal parts molasses and honey mixed together. Some pediatricians recommend honey as a laxative for babies because it is so mild.

ULCERS

Hippocrates, the great Greek physician and father of modern medicine, recommended honey as a cure for ulcers.

SWELLING

Potato poultice:

Relieve swelling with an easy-to-make potato poultice. Grate a potato or soak the skin of a white potato in vinegar. Wrap in a clean cloth and apply, and swelling will soon be alleviated.

TEETH AND GUMS

CRACKED TEETH

Your teeth can crack with abrupt temperature changes, so don't, for example, take a sip of ice water and then take a sip of tea. With a little conscious effort at the beginning, it should become automatic for you to avoid such changes. Once the teeth develop hairline cracks, there is nothing that can be done about them.

TO WHITEN TEETH

Lemon peel cleans and bleaches. Use some (the yellow outside part) to clean and whiten your teeth, then do the same for your sink, and last, let it clean out your garbage disposal.

Baking-soda toothpaste:
Sprinkle some baking soda into the palm of your nonbrushing hand, add water to make a loose paste, and brush. Teeth come out as white as with any product on the market, at a fraction of the cost. It will also not wear away the enamel.

Hydrogen peroxide brushed on your teeth with a toothbrush will whiten them.

Used as a mouthwash, it will kill bacteria. Rinse mouth out thoroughly with water afterward, because hyrdogen peroxide is poisonous if swallowed. In tiny amounts, such as what might be left after these uses, it will do no harm.

The Victorians used sodium perborate to whiten both their teeth and their clothes. It comes in a powder, which one mixes with water. To whiten teeth, make a paste and rinse off after only a few seconds. For clothes, let the item soak overnight in this solution.

The Costume Institute at the Metropolitan Museum of Art in New York uses this old Victorian technique to whiten old clothes without harming them.

TOOTHBRUSHES

Natural toothbrush:

Strip the bark from twigs of a dogwood tree and rub the ends against the teeth and gently around the gums. It will stimulate the gums and leave teeth shining white.

This is an old tradition among southern blacks and the people of the West Indies.

To sterilize a toothbrush, dampen the brush and sprinkle a layer of salt on it, then let it dry.

GUMS

A dentist friend says that if everyone got plenty of vitamin C and rinsed their mouth daily with salt water, dentists would be out of business. This is particularly recommended for gum problems.

Gum problems? Stimulate the circulation and thereby their health by squeezing and massaging the gums near the teeth, using two fingers, one finger inside and the other outside the teeth.

The same method is recommended for a tooth that aches (until you get to the dentist).

TOOTHACHES

For a toothache:

Dip a piece of cotton into some rum or brandy and hold it in your mouth against the tooth. It will make you feel better until you get to the dentist.

This also works for new teeth coming through the gums, like wisdom teeth. For a teething baby, dab the liquor on with your finger.

Toothache be gone:

Heat 1 tablespoon honey, add 5 whole cloves, and stir. When the mixture is warm, remove the cloves and chew them slowly and gently, rolling them around the aching area.

Eat pineapple before you have a tooth pulled. The swelling will go down more quickly.

After a tooth is pulled, dentists recommend holding a Lipton teabag, moistened and wrapped in soft cloth or a paper towel, against the bleeding gum to stop the bleeding quickly.

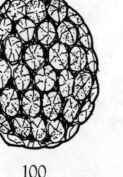

VAGINITIS

For vaginitis or Trichomonas, soak 3 cloves garlic in ½ half cup distilled white vinegar for 8 to 10 hours. Throw away the garlic cloves, and use 3 tablespoons of the vinegar with 1 pint warm water in a douche. Douche every 3 to 4 hours.

For Trichomonas, wrap a peeled and un-nicked garlic clove in a piece of sterile gauze. Tie the gauze in such a way that a string will hang out when you insert this homemade suppository in the vagina. Leave it in for several hours, then replace the whole thing with a fresh one. This might have to be continued for a week.

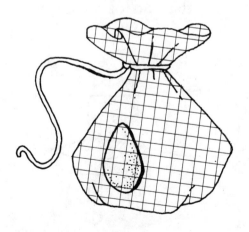

VARICOSE VEINS

Witch hazel pack:

For relief and to reduce the swelling and constriction of varicose veins, North American Indians used to make a poultice with witch hazel. Soak a bandage in extract of witch hazel and wrap around varicose veins. Lie down with feet slightly raised for a half hour.

Another way to shrink varicose veins comes from folk medicine traditions of Sweden, Scotland, England, and Germany:

Apply straight apple cider vinegar to the veins each night and morning. Also take 2 teaspoons of the vinegar in a glass of water twice a day. The veins should have shrunk noticeably by the end of a month.

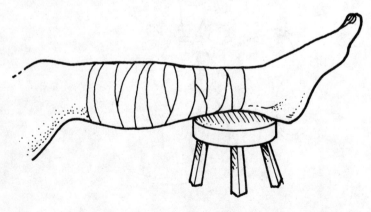

FEELING GOOD

This section contains hints that are not so much for specific ailments, but more for overall good health, the kind of well-being that makes it difficult for illness to take hold. Sleep is important, since if one sleeps well, the body is more resistant to disease. In the same way, if you are more wide awake when up, you sleep better at night. If you can conquer disturbing dreams, you get more rest while sleeping.

Then there are some things that make you feel luxurious and pampered, like scented baths and oils. And it is not only music that hath charms, but also color, great smells, learning to relax, and the triumphant feeling that comes from kicking bad habits or losing weight. All these can make you feel good.

BATH HERBS

Water has a deeply relaxing and powerful therapeutic effect, and bathing herbs can enhance all the benefits. Since herbs have different properties, mixtures can be made to calm and relax, rejuvenate and stimulate, or simply smell delicious. Here are several combinations that can be made ahead of time and stored in attractive jars just waiting for the right occasion. To use, place a large handful of herb mixture in a cotton bag and tie to the faucet, letting the water run into the tub through the bag. Each bag can be reused three or four times.

Calming and Relaxing Formula:
    2 parts camomile
    1 part linden flowers
    1 part mistletoe
    1 part violet leaves

Stimulating and Rejuvenating Formulas:
    Equal parts lavender, peppermint, comfrey leaf, comfrey root, and lemon verbena.
    Sage, patchouli leaf, sandalwood chips, lemon thyme, eucalyptus, or bay leaves.
    Peppermint or spearmint, camomile, roses, rosemary, comfrey root, bay leaves.

Scented Blossom Formulas:
    For oily skin use equal parts witch hazel bark, lemon peel, white-oak bark, peppermint, orange flowers or orange peel, or

Raspberry leaf, strawberry leaf,
lemon grass, lemon peel, and
camomile flowers.

For dry skin use equal amounts
comfrey leaf, comfrey root,
camomile, roses, rosemary.
Acacia, camomile, violets (leaves and
flowers), and roses.

Make wonderfully smelling herbal bouquets.
Here is one for the bath:
Tie into a cloth some dried or fresh leaves
of orange, rosemary, or eucalyptus.

BATH SALTS

These are used for both softness and scent.
You may vary this recipe slightly, depending
on available ingredients.

1 cup borax
⅛ cup kelp powder
⅛ cup ground oatmeal
⅛ cup sea salt

Place ingredients in a jar and sprinkle with
your favorite essential oil. Allow to dry for a
few hours, then mix well, making sure that
any lumps are smoothed out. Store in a jar
with a snugly fitting lid and use 4 tablespoons to a bath.

BUBBLE BATH RECIPE

3 tablespoons liquid shampoo
2 cups vegetable oil
10 drops perfume

Beat in blender set at high speed for a few minutes and enjoy your next bath.

BATH OIL

Pour baby oil into your bathwater to soften skin.

OATMEAL BATH

For sensitive skin, a rash, or just to give your skin a treat, take a small handful of oatmeal and tie it securely into a cheesecloth bag or a sock. Moisten and use exactly as you would soap.

The oatmeal bag can be used two or three times if it is thoroughly dried out after use by hanging in an airy place.

Put the bag into your bathwater for all-over luxury.

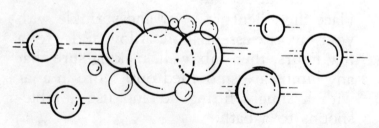

AFTER THE BATH

Powders:

Here are some varieties of dusting powders that are made ahead of time and stored. They are free of irritants.

> 1 cup finely powdered white clay
> ¼ cup finely powdered oatmeal
> ¼ cup finely powdered orris root

Add any one of the following for a variety of scents: finely powdered roses, lavender, camomile, sandalwood, cedar, patchouli leaves, lemon peel, or cinnamon.

Mix ingredients thoroughly, sprinkle with essential oil to match powdered blossoms, dry, and remove any lumps before storing.

Cornstarch makes a perfectly good body and face powder.

Moisten a handful of salt and rub it all over the body. Rinse off and dry quickly. It certainly feels refreshing, but whether it will relieve nervousness, as some turn-of-the-century Americans believed, is more doubtful.

BREATHING

Alternate nostril breathing is a yoga technique to regulate the breath and bring feelings of peace and relaxation.

Place your right thumb lightly against your right nostril. Place your ring and little finger lightly against your left nostril. Exhale slowly through both nostrils.

Next, press your right nostril closed and slowly inhale deeply through your left nostril to a count of five. Keeping your right nostril closed, press the left one closed. Hold the air in your lungs to a count of five. Open your right nostril and exhale through it to a count of five. Without pausing, repeat, but this time begin with the now open right nostril.

Repeat entire cycle for five to ten minutes.

CIRCULATION IN THE LEGS

Lie down and elevate the legs above the rest of the body and relax, breathing deeply. Done every day for five to fifteen minutes at a time, the circulation of blood in the legs will be aided. Many older people have serious trouble with their legs; this simple tip will help avoid these troubles.

A variation that is also good for the back is to lie on the floor, back completely flat against the floor, the legs from hips to knees pointing at the ceiling. The legs from knees to ankles rest on the seat of a chair.

DEPRESSION

The ancient Greeks believed that eating honey could cure bad moods and sour personalities.

You might want to take this remedy, from a booklet put out by the Diamond Crystal Salt Company in 1925, with a grain of salt:

"A pinch of Diamond Crystal Salt allowed to dissolve in the mouth will relieve that depressed feeling and serve as a tonic."

DIETING

Squeeze your earlobe to depress the appetite.

Vermont folk medicine holds that apple cider vinegar mixed with water will help burn off fat. The remedy suggests two teaspoons to a glass of water taken at the end of each meal.

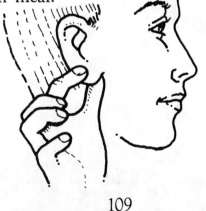

An interesting list compiled by the Pasadena
Arts Society.

To burn 100 calories:

      Run 1550 yards in 7 minutes
      Bicycle 2 miles in 9 minutes
      Swim 400 yards in 9 minutes
      Play tennis 14 minutes
      Walk 1500 yards in 20 minutes
      Bowl for 22 minutes

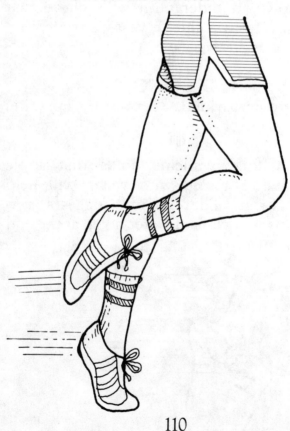

ENERGY

For a between-meal energy booster, drink a glass of fruit juice into which 1 or 2 tablespoons of honey has been mixed.

This healthy aperitif is heartily recommended by a woman from the Netherlands:

To a bottle of noncarbonated mineral water, add 1 tablespoon quinine powder, 1 tablespoon powdered cinnamon, ½ cup honey, and ¼ cup cider vinegar. Let stand for twenty-four hours. Serve ice cold.

MUSIC

Music hath charms to soothe the savage beast? One of the best is Johann Pachelbel's Canon in D, also called the Immortal Canon. Used as the theme in the film *Ordinary People*, it will aid relaxation and diminish headaches.

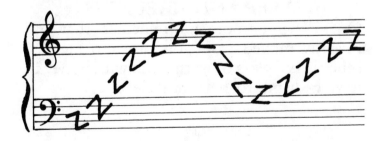

The vibrations caused by some sounds have long been known to have a healing effect. Here is a process that many people have found draws healing sounds out of their own bodies:

> 1. Stand or sit with the back straight; hold the head so the spine of the neck is also straight. Close the eyes.

> 2. Let long sounds out of your body. Imagine sound traveling up from the feet, moving through the body, maybe getting stuck in certain places until the sound melts the blocks. Keep feeling the sounds and their movement.

> 3. Let the sound move upward until it goes out the top of the head, at which point a sigh signals the end of the process.

SLEEP AND TIREDNESS

One of grandmother's remedies that has recently moved from folklore into medical schools is a glass of warm milk with honey in it at bedtime to help one sleep.

A teaspoon or two of honey can bring on the sandman. If you're having trouble sleeping at night, here's an easy remedy. Add 3 teaspoons apple cider vinegar to a cup of honey. Just before going to bed, take 2 teaspoonsful. You should be asleep within a half hour. If not, repeat the dosage.

One folk remedy is better than a sleeping pill:

Mix together in a small cloth bag 3 ounces rose petals, 2 ounces mint leaves, and ½ an ounce powdered cloves. Sew up tight—or tie with a pretty ribbon—and place it under your pillow to sleep, sleep, sleep.

To help you wake up more completely in the morning, or as a freshener during the day, rub some rosemary oil or rosemary cologne into the skin at pulse points (such as wrists, temples, between the eyes and the ears, on the throat). Being more awake during the day promotes better sleeping at night.

The Chinese brought this tip with them to the United States:

Slap the insides of the elbows and knees where "tiredness collects."

SMELLS

Potpourris started as masks for obnoxious odors because bad smells were associated with disease. Today, however, they are marketed as a sweet-smelling item of home decor. You needn't go out and purchase a potpourri. They're easy enough to make at home from supplies on hand in your kitchen.

One of my favorites combines the dried, sliced peel of 2 oranges; 4 sticks of cinnamon, crumbled; 12 whole cloves; and a teaspoon of rosemary. Cap and seal well until ready to use. When uncovered, the smell will be heavenly. Put in little bags in closets or drawers, or just uncover to make a whole room smell good.

From the Deep South comes this tip:

Use a touch of vanilla behind your ears as you would perfume. People are haunted by the familiarity of the smell but rarely recognize it.

Breathing cigarette smoke has been proven to be bad for you, even if the cigarette is smoked by someone else. If you cannot keep cigarette smokers out of your house entirely, the next best thing is to burn candles in the room. A burning candle will absorb the smoke.

Burning a candle will also absorb the smells from slicing onions and garlic.

ıllı

If a skunk sprays you with its distinctive odor, bathe in tomato juice to remove the smell.

ıllı

SMOKING

Warnings against the evils of smoking have prevailed for a long time. Around the turn of the century, cures for kicking the habit abounded. Here are a few that, at least in some cases, resemble present-day coping techniques.

ıllı

It used to be recommended that one go on a diet of fruit juices and vegetable broths for eight to fifteen days. Today we suggest drinking multiple glasses of water and nibbling on small tidbits of fruits and vegetables.

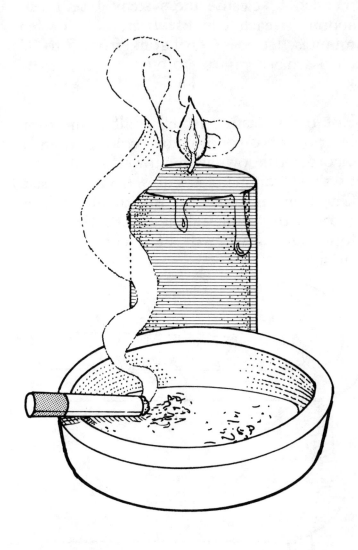

A strong red-clover tea was also recommended to cleanse the system. Use 1 teaspoon to each cup of water, boil for ten minutes, let steep, and drink from 5 to 12 cups a day.

Hot baths, lasting from a half hour to an hour or more, followed by a cold spray and a vigorous rubdown with a towel, are also part of the recommended cures from the past. One thing is certain: it *is* difficult to keep tobacco dry while taking a bath. At least a long daily bath will help cut down on smoking.

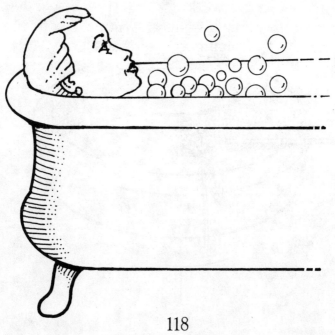

HARD TO CLASSIFY

BLOOD TYPE

Write your blood type on your driver's license. If you are in an accident, it could save your life.

EXAMS

Exam time special:

Eat sunflower or sesame seeds to improve memory and concentration.

ACHES AND PAINS

A superb cook we know uses a steamer to heat cloths for hot applications for pain, instead of wringing out the cloths in hot water.

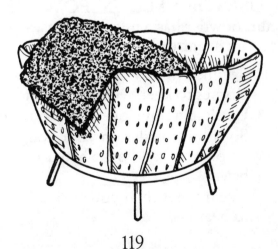

As soon as you feel a sprain, strain, or break, doctors recommend **RICE:**

R = **rest:** The injury might be made worse if you continue to use the injured part.

I = **ice:** Apply ice immediately to reduce hemorrhaging.

C = **compression:** Put pressure on the wound to reduce swelling, usually with an Ace bandage.

E = **elevation:** Keep the injured part above the level of the heart, so gravity will drain excess fluid.

Call the doctor if the injury seems sufficiently severe.

USES OF TALCUM POWDER

Talcum powder has a number of uses beyond its use as an after-bath powder:

> Sprinkle it in your shoes and sports clothes to keep feeling cool and fresh.
> Use it as a translucent face powder.
> Sprinkle powder on your body to help brush sand off when leaving the beach.
> Use frequently if you are susceptible to heat rash.

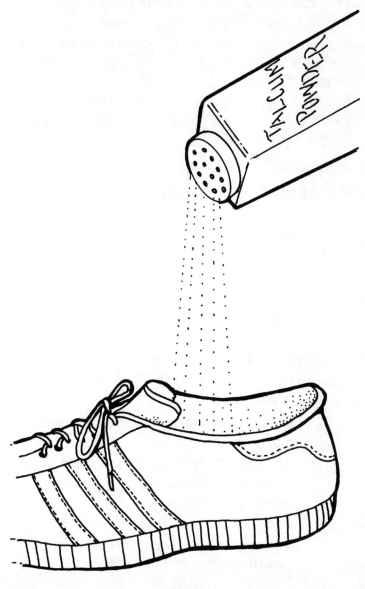

USES OF GARLIC

For centuries garlic has been known as a healing herb. Thanks to its delicious taste it is easy to increase its use in almost any diet, and one of the breath fresheners mentioned elsewhere in this book, such as parsley or a lemon slice with salt on it or caraway seeds, eaten at the end of the meal, will take care of garlic breath.

Following is a list of the benefits for which it is most frequently mentioned.

> It aids digestion.
> As a sweat promoter, it is good at the onset of colds, coughs, and sore throats.
> It kills bacteria.
> Browned in honey and butter, it is good for bladder and kidney disorders.
> It stimulates energy.
> It alleviates arthritis and other muscle and joint pains.
> For hypertensive patients, it opens blood vessels and thereby reduces blood pressure.
> It is good for sinus troubles.
> Some success has been reported in deworming people and dogs.

USES OF GLYCERINE

Glycerine, available at the drugstore in small bottles, is one of those multipurpose wonders. It is not only good for chapped lips, but it even tastes good. Put in the back of your throat, it will heal a sore throat more quickly. It speeds the healing of scrapes and cuts and makes a great moisturizer for the face. All this and inexpensive, too.

CHICKEN SOUP

Another remedy that has recently moved from folklore into the medical schools is chicken soup for just about any illness. It has been found that chicken soup restores the electrolytes that are lost during illness.

LIST OF SOURCES

Ingredients that are unavailable locally may be obtained by mail order from the following sources:

Aphrodisia Products, Inc.
28 Carmine Street
New York, N.Y. 10014

Capriland's Herb Farm
Silver Street
Coventry, Conn. 06238

Caswell-Massey Co., Ltd.
575 Lexington Ave.
New York, N.Y. 10022

Haussmann's Pharmacy
534-536 West Girard Ave.
Philadelphia, Pa. 19123

Herbarium, Inc.
Route 2, Box 620
Kenosha, Wis. 53140

Herbs N' Honey Nursery
c/o Mrs. Chester Fisher
Route 2, Box 205
Monmouth, Ore. 97361

Hickory Hollow
Route 1, Box 52
Peterstown, W. Va. 24963

Indiana Botanic Gardens, Inc.
P.O. Box 5
Hammond, Ind. 46325

Meadowbrook Herb Garden
Wyoming, R.I. 02898

Nature's Herb Co.
281 Ellis Street
San Francisco, Cal. 94102

Nichols Garden Nursery
1190 N. Pacific Highway
Albany, Ore. 97321

Old Fashioned Herb Co.
P.O. Box 1000-G
Springfield, Utah 84663

Penn Herb Co.
603 N. Second Street
Philadelphia, Pa. 19123

Well-Sweep Herb Farm
317 Mount Bethel Road
Port Murray, N.J. 07865

Wide World of Herbs, Ltd.
P.O. Box 266
Rouses Point, N.Y. 12979

In England:
   Culpeper Ltd.
   Hadstock Road
   Linton
   Cambridge CB1 6NJ, England

In Canada:
   Wide World of Herbs, Ltd.
   11 Sainte Catherine Street East
   Montreal, Quebec
   Canada H2X 1K3

The information in this book is not intended to be prescriptive or to replace the advice of a physician. Anyone using medication or under the care of a doctor for serious illness should consult with him or her before using these remedies. The author and publisher assume no legal responsibility for the advice and information contained herein. This book is intended to serve as an informative publication for the use of the general public.

SHARE YOUR FAVORITE HINTS WITH US.

Send to:
HOME REMEDIES
PERIGEE BOOKS
200 Madison Avenue
New York, NY 10016

No purchase is necessary to qualify.
Simply send in your original hints.
If they are used in forthcoming sequels of
Home Remedies
you will be notified and sent a free copy
of our next great book of home remedies.

Submission of *Home Remedies* by readers
constitutes your permission for accepted hints
to be published in any *Home Remedies* sequel.